Great Desserts

by Christine Koury

BARRON'S
Woodbury, New York • London • Toronto • Sydney

Great Desserts

by Christine Koury

BARRON'S
Woodbury, New York • London • Toronto • Sydney

All inquiries should be addressed to:

Barron's Educational Series, Inc.
113 Crossways Park Drive
Woodbury, New York 11797

International Standard Book
No. 0-8120-5590-X
Library of Congress Catalog Card
No. 84-6489

**Library of Congress Cataloging
in Publication Data**
Koury, Christine.
  Great desserts.

  (Easy cooking series)
  Includes index.
  1. Desserts. I. Title. II. Series.
TX773.K65 1984   641.8′6   84-6489
ISBN 0-8120-5590-X

PRINTED IN HONG KONG
4 5 6 7   9 8 7 6 5 4 3 2 1

Credits

Photography
Color photographs: Matthew Klein
Food styling: Andrea Swenson
Photo stylist: Linda Cheverton
Photo Accessories: china from Villeroy & Boch,
  New York; crystal from Waterford, New York;
  flowers by Cathy Sviba at Hortiflora, New
  York; silver by Cristofle from Baccarat, New
  York.

Author Christine Koury is the food editor
  for *Woman's World,* and has been developing
  and testing recipes for several years.

Cover and book design Milton Glaser, Inc.
Series editor Carole Berglie

INTRODUCTION

When you're looking for a dessert, there's no need to search any further. Whether you want something simple or spectacular, you can find the perfect ending to any meal. All of these delicious treats are simple to make, but will satisfy even the choosiest dessert lover. Some are rich and creamy, some are light and refreshing, some plain, some fancy, but all are irresistible!

Plan dessert to go with your meal. Serve something light like Cranberry Orange Sorbet after a hearty meal; after a lighter meal, serve something rich and sinful like the Coconut Meringues filled with Chocolate Mousse.

All these desserts were developed for the cook who likes to have something to show, yet really doesn't have the time to spend hours in the kitchen "slaving" over a hot stove. They can be prepared in about 30 minutes or less, although some will need several hours to cook, then cool, freeze, or set. (That's time that you have free, since you don't have to be in the kitchen.)

Just about everyone loves desserts and looks forward to them at the end of dinner. Watch the faces light up as soon as the word is mentioned. Whether it's a humble treat such as Peach and Plum Crumble or a more impressive finale such as the fabulous yet simple Layered Baked Alaska, you're sure to get smiles at the end.

If you're looking for dazzling desserts without the work that goes with them, try the Ice Cream Bombe or the Frozen Strawberry Colada Soufflé. Both are made ahead, so if you are entertaining there's no last-minute rushing around to prepare them.

If fruit is your passion, the Blueberry, Peaches and Cream Tart, the Ginger-glazed Fruit Salad, or the Poached Pears with Cognac Sauce will make your mouth water.

For chocolate lovers, there are such temptations as the Three-layer Brownies, a Chocolate Pound Cake layered with whipped cream, a French Silk Pie that's made with white chocolate, the Chocolate Bread Pudding, and an all-time favorite, Chocolate Cake with Chocolate Icing.

Quick and easy last-minute desserts don't have to be a problem. Creations such as Sautéed Bananas served over pound cake or ice cream or Zabaglione over luscious fresh fruit are nice endings to any meal or evening. They're so simple to make yet special enough to stand on their own if you want a late-night dessert to highlight a special occasion.

Your kids will love the Toffee Nut Bars as extra-special treats in their lunchboxes, and they'll look forward to afternoon snacks when it's an Ice Cream Sandwich made with oatmeal cookies.

Making your own desserts is gratifying. The end results put store-bought desserts to shame and you'll never resort to them again. Once you see how much pleasure you give your family, your friends, and yourself, you won't want to settle for anything less than homemade.

GENERAL HINTS AND BASIC SKILLS

Here are some tips to make your desserts successful:

● Before beginning any recipe, read it completely before starting—both the list of ingredients and the preparation. Check to be sure that you have all the necessary ingredients on hand before you start. Don't take it for granted that you have everything on the shelf (baking soda, baking powder, spices, etc.). You don't want to be halfway through the recipe and realize that you only have one egg but need three to make the dessert. Measure out the correct amount of ingredients before you begin.

● Any dessert with a custard or cream base or filling must be refrigerated.

● When making a cake, have ingredients at room temperature. Take eggs, liquid (such as milk), and butter from refrigerator about one hour before beginning. If eggs need to be separated for the recipe, separate them while they are cold, then let the separated yolks and whites come to room temperature. Cover yolks so they don't dry out.

● Greasing and flouring cake pans prevents the cakes from sticking to the pans. Grease the bottom and sides with an even layer of softened butter, margarine, or solid vegetable shortening. Sprinkle a small amount of flour in the bottom of the pan and shake around the pan until sides and bottom are coated. Turn pan over and tap lightly to remove the excess flour.

● Use the correct size pan called for in a cake recipe. If the pan is too small, the cake may overflow and be compact. If the pan is too large, it may not rise properly and brown unevenly.

● It is very important when baking that your oven is accurate. Keeping an oven thermometer in your oven while baking is a good way to be sure. You will know right away if your oven needs an adjustment.

● When baking in glass pans instead of metal, reduce the oven temperature in recipe by 25 degrees.

● When baking, place pans in the center of the oven. If you have more than one pan, they should not touch each other or the sides of the oven. If both pans do not fit on one shelf, stagger them on the two middle shelves.

● Measure all ingredients accurately; it is a must for successful results, especially in baking.

MEASURING INGREDIENTS

For measuring *dry* ingredients, use either plastic or metal nested measuring cups. Spoon the ingredient into the correct size cup and level it off with the flat edge of a spatula or knife. Do not try to level flour by shaking the measuring cup; this will pack the flour.

For measuring *liquid* ingredients, use either a glass or plastic measuring cup with a spout. The cup should have markings on the outside. Check the correct mark of measurement at eye level.

Measuring spoons should be from 1/4 teaspoon to 1 tablespoon. They may be made either of plastic or metal. Fill the correct spoon size to overflowing with dry ingredients. With straight edge, level off ingredient so that it is level with the spoon. Measuring spoons are also used to measure liquid ingredients that are less than 1/4 cup. Anything above 1/4 cup is measured in a liquid measuring cup.

- **Equivalents**
  3 teaspoons = 1 tablespoon
  16 tablespoons = 1 cup
  1 cup = 8 fluid ounces
  2 cups = 1 pint
  2 pints = 1 quart
  4 cups = 1 quart

INGREDIENTS

- **Eggs** Use *large* eggs unless recipe calls for another size. Separate eggs directly from the refrigerator—there is less chance that the yolk will break. For whites to whip, there can't be any trace of yolk or any other fat. Be sure that all equipment is clean. When separating eggs, break each egg into a small bowl first. Separate it and then add the white to the other separated whites and the yolk to the other separated yolks. This way if you break one yolk while separating eggs, you will not get the yolk into the rest of the whites.

- **Butter** When a recipe calls for butter (or cream cheese) at room temperature, it is because softened butter is easier to work with and will become smooth and creamy instead of lumpy when beaten. These recipes call for butter so that the final product has a nice buttery flavor. If you prefer to use margarine, use stick margarine, not the soft kind that comes in a tub.

- **Flour** These recipes call for all-purpose flour, measured after sifting. Since most major brands of all-purpose flour are now presifted, you need not sift before measuring.

- **Sugar, cocoa** Before adding brown sugar to a recipe, break up any large lumps. Also, if using cocoa or confectioners sugar and it has lumps, sift to remove the lumps before adding it to the rest of the ingredients.

- **Cream** When whipping cream, chill the bowl and beaters for a few minutes and make sure that the cream is very cold. That way, the whipped cream will be lighter. Whip the cream in a high, narrow bowl to avoid spattering. When the cream has reached the point at which soft peaks begin to form, decrease whipping speed so that you will not overbeat it.

- **Pastry** When working with puff pastry, make sure that the pastry remains cool. If the butter between the layers is allowed to soften, the pastry will become greasy when cooked. If the pastry starts to become soft while you are working with it, put it back into the refrigerator until it is firm again. Try not to stretch the pastry when you are working with it.

ABOUT THE RECIPE ANALYSES

For each recipe in this book, you'll note that we have provided data on the quantities of protein, fat, sodium, carbohydrates, and potassium, as well as the number of calories (kcal) per serving. If you are on a low-calorie diet or are watching your intake of sodium, for example, these figures should help you gauge your eating habits and help you balance your meals. Bear in mind, however, that the calculations are fundamentally estimates, and are to be followed only in a very general way. All the figures will vary somewhat depending on the size of the portions you serve.

YIELD

8 servings

Per serving
calories 467, protein 6 g,
fat 26 g, sodium 327 mg,
carbohydrates 54 g,
potassium 188 mg

TIME

20 minutes preparation
1 hour cooking
1 hour cooling

INGREDIENTS

½ cup butter, at room temperature
1 cup granulated sugar
4 eggs
1 teaspoon vanilla extract
1 tablespoon instant coffee powder
¼ cup boiling water
1 cup all-purpose flour
½ cup unsweetened cocoa
1 teaspoon baking soda
½ teaspoon salt

FILLING

7 tablespoons apricot preserves
1 cup heavy cream
1 tablespoon confectioners sugar
¼ teaspoon vanilla extract

Preheat oven to 325 degrees. Grease and flour a 9½ × 5½-inch loaf pan ①. In medium bowl, cream butter and sugar. Beat in eggs and vanilla. Stir coffee into boiling water until dissolved. Beat into creamed mixture along with flour, cocoa, baking soda, and salt. Turn into prepared pan and bake 50 to 60 minutes until a cake tester inserted in center comes out clean. Cool on wire rack in pan for 10 minutes. Remove from pan and cool completely on wire rack 50 minutes.

When cake is cooled, slice horizontally into 3 layers ②. Stir apricot preserves until smooth. Spread the bottom and middle layers each with 3 tablespoons apricot preserves ③. Beat cream with sugar and vanilla until stiff. Spread ¼ cup whipped cream over each of the layers with the apricot preserves. Stack layers and top with remaining layer of cake. Spread sides and top with whipped cream. Drizzle remaining apricot preserves over whipped cream.

YIELD

10 servings

Per serving
calories 260, protein 4 g,
fat 15 g, sodium 142 mg,
carbohydrates 30 g,
potassium 220 mg

TIME

30 minutes preparation
4 to 6 hours freezing

INGREDIENTS

½ cup shelled almonds
⅔ cup graham cracker crumbs
2 tablespoons granulated sugar
¼ cup butter, melted

FILLING

1 pint vanilla ice cream
1 package (10 ounces) frozen
  raspberries in syrup, thawed
1 pint peach ice cream (see note)
1¼ teaspoons cornstarch
1 peach, sliced (optional)
¼ cup fresh raspberries (optional)

In blender or food processor, process almonds until finely ground. In a small bowl, stir together ground almonds, graham cracker crumbs, sugar, and melted butter until combined. Press into a 9-inch pie dish ①.

Let vanilla ice cream soften slightly. Drain raspberries, reserving syrup. Spoon vanilla ice cream into pie dish and spread until smooth ②; top with raspberries; freeze 1 hour.

Let peach ice cream soften slightly. Spread in pie dish over raspberries ③. Cover and freeze several hours until firm.

For sauce, stir cornstarch into 1 tablespoon of the syrup drained from raspberries. Place remaining syrup (⅔ cup) in small saucepan. Stir in cornstarch mixture. Cook over low heat, stirring constantly until slightly thickened. Chill at least 1 hour.

To serve pie, let stand about 20 minutes at room temperature. Garnish with peach slices and fresh raspberries. Serve with sauce.

NOTE If peach ice cream is unavailable, 1 cup chopped peaches may be stirred into 1 pint vanilla ice cream and substituted for peach ice cream.

CINNAMON CHEESECAKE

YIELD

10 servings

Per serving
calories 413, protein 7 g,
fat 26 g, sodium 233 mg,
carbohydrates 37 g,
potassium 146 mg

TIME

10 minutes preparation
1 hour, 10 minutes
   cooking
5 hours setting

INGREDIENTS

1¼ cups granola
16 ounces cream cheese, at room
   temperature
1 cup granulated sugar
1 tablespoon vanilla extract
1 teaspoon ground cinnamon
¼ teaspoon salt
4 eggs
½ cup heavy cream
1 cup cherry pie filling

Preheat oven to 350 degrees. Sprinkle granola into bottom of an 8-inch springform pan. Bake 10 minutes. Reduce oven to 300 degrees. In large bowl, beat cream cheese until smooth. Beat in sugar, vanilla, cinnamon, and salt. Add eggs and heavy cream and beat until combined. Pour into springform pan ①. Bake 1 hour. Turn oven off and leave cake in oven, without opening door, 1 hour.

Remove cake from oven and let cool to room temperature. Remove side of pan ②. Spread cherry pie filling over top ③ and refrigerate several hours.

YIELD

8 turnovers

Per turnover
calories 341, protein 3 g,
fat 22 g, sodium 254 mg,
carbohydrates 33 g,
potassium 134 mg

TIME

20 minutes preparation
25 minutes cooking
30 minutes cooling

INGREDIENTS

1 package (17¼ ounces) frozen puff
   pastry
2 large apples
¼ teaspoon vanilla extract
2 tablespoons light brown sugar
¼ teaspoon ground cinnamon
⅓ cup raisins
1½ teaspoons granulated sugar
Pinch of ground cinnamon
1 tablespoon milk

Thaw pastry according to package directions. Preheat oven to 375 degrees. While pastry is thawing, pare, core, and chop apples. Sprinkle with vanilla and mix. Stir together brown sugar and cinnamon. Add apples and raisins to sugar mixture and toss to coat apples evenly with mixture.

On lightly floured surface, unfold pastry. Cut each sheet into quarters. Place about ⅛ cup apple mixture onto each piece of pastry ①. Fold pastry in half over apple mixture, forming a triangle ②. Press edges together and, using fork tines, seal closed ③. Make 3 small slices in top of each for vent.

Mix sugar and pinch of cinnamon. Brush each turnover with milk and sprinkle lightly with cinnamon sugar. Bake on very lightly greased baking sheet about 25 minutes until lightly browned. Cool on wire racks.

YIELD

8 servings

Per serving (without sauce)
calories 327, protein 4 g, fat 21 g, sodium 102 mg, carbohydrates 30 g, potassium 237 mg

TIME

20 minutes preparation
5½ hours freezing

INGREDIENTS

1 quart coffee ice cream
1 pint chocolate ice cream
¾ cup heavy cream
1 tablespoon confectioners sugar
2 tablespoons creme de cacao
1 ounce semisweet chocolate, chopped
Hot fudge sauce

Place a 7-cup ice cream mold in freezer. Place coffee ice cream in refrigerator about 20 minutes or until slightly softened. Remove mold from freezer and ice cream from refrigerator. Stir coffee ice cream until smooth and spread into mold, leaving a well in center ①. Place in freezer for 1 hour or until firm.

Place chocolate ice cream in refrigerator about 10 minutes or until slightly softened; stir until smooth. Spread over coffee ice cream in mold, leaving a well in center. Freeze 1 hour or until firm.

Whip cream with sugar until stiff. Fold in creme de cacao, then chopped chocolate. Spoon into center of mold. Freeze 3 hours or until firm.

To remove bombe from mold, place a warm damp cloth over mold 10 seconds. Run a knife around edge ②. Place a plate on bottom of mold and invert. Lift off mold ③. Serve with hot fudge sauce.

YIELD

6 servings

Per serving
calories 397, protein 4 g,
fat 11 g, sodium 109 mg,
carbohydrates 73 g,
potassium 534 mg

TIME

20 minutes preparation
40 to 45 minutes cooking

INGREDIENTS

2½ pounds peaches or nectarines
1 pound plums
⅓ cup granulated sugar
⅓ cup firmly packed light brown
   sugar
¼ cup all-purpose flour
¼ teaspoon ground cinnamon
1 tablespoon lemon juice

CRUMBLE TOPPING

¾ cup old-fashioned rolled oats
⅓ cup all-purpose flour
¼ cup firmly packed light brown
   sugar
¼ teaspoon ground cinnamon
⅓ cup butter, melted

Drop peaches into boiling water for about 30 seconds. Remove and place under cold running water until cooled. Peel off skin ①. Preheat oven to 375 degrees. Cut peaches and plums into slices and remove pits ②.

In large bowl, stir together granulated sugar, brown sugar, flour, and cinnamon. Toss fruit with lemon juice, then toss with sugar mixture. Place in 9½-inch oval baking dish (6 cups) ③.

In small bowl, stir together oats, flour, brown sugar, and cinnamon. Stir in butter. Sprinkle over fruit. Place dish on baking sheet. Bake 40 to 45 minutes until fruit is tender.

7

YIELD

20 brownies

Per brownie
calories 313, protein 4 g,
fat 15 g, sodium 131 mg,
carbohydrates 42 g,
potassium 123 mg

TIME

20 minutes preparation
35 to 40 minutes cooking
1 hour cooling

INGREDIENTS

3 ounces unsweetened chocolate
⅔ cup butter
3 eggs
1½ cups granulated sugar
2 teaspoons vanilla extract
1 cup all-purpose flour

BUTTERSCOTCH LAYER

¼ cup butter, at room temperature
3 ounces cream cheese, at room temperature
1 cup firmly packed dark brown sugar
2 eggs
2 teaspoons vanilla extract
⅔ cup all-purpose flour

ICING

1 ounce unsweetened chocolate
2 tablespoons butter
1 cup confectioners sugar
2 tablespoons milk

Preheat oven to 375 degrees. Grease and flour a 9 × 13-inch pan. Melt chocolate and butter over low heat. In medium bowl, beat eggs, sugar and vanilla. Beat in melted chocolate mixture ①. Stir in flour until well combined.

For butterscotch layer, beat butter and cream cheese until smooth; beat in brown sugar. Beat in eggs and vanilla. Stir in flour.

Spread brownies into pan. Pour butterscotch mixture over brownies and spread evenly ②. Bake 35 to 40 minutes; cool on wire rack.

For icing, melt chocolate and butter over low heat. In small bowl, stir together confectioners sugar and milk until smooth. Stir in melted chocolate mixture. Spread over brownies ③ and set aside until set. Cut into bars.

YIELD

10 servings

Per serving
calories 210, protein 2 g,
fat 13 g, sodium 131 mg,
carbohydrates 19 g,
potassium 100 mg

TIME

25 minutes preparation
10 to 15 minutes cooking
2½ hours chilling

INGREDIENTS

1 package (17¼ ounces) frozen puff
    pastry (will only use 1 sheet)
1 egg yolk
1 teaspoon water
½ teaspoon granulated sugar

FILLING

3 ounces cream cheese, at room
    temperature
1 tablespoon light brown sugar
1 tablespoon granulated sugar

½ teaspoon vanilla extract
⅓ cup sour cream

FRUIT AND GLAZE

2 peaches or nectarines
¼ cup apricot preserves
½ cup blueberries

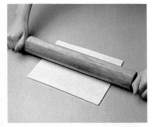

Thaw 1 sheet of puff pastry according to package directions. On lightly floured surface, roll pastry into a 10-inch square ①. Cut two 1-inch strips from the bottom. Brush a 1-inch strip of pastry, on both the top and the bottom of the rectangle, with water. Lay strips of pastry over water and press lightly to attach ②. Beat egg yolk and water. Brush over pastry strips and sprinkle with sugar. Prick bottom of pastry (not strips) in several places ③. Chill 30 minutes.

Preheat oven to 400 degrees. Bake pastry on lightly greased baking sheet, 10 to 15 minutes until lightly browned. Press down center of pastry if puffed. Remove to wire rack to cool.

Beat cream cheese until smooth. Beat in brown sugar, granulated sugar, and vanilla. Stir in sour cream. Spread on cooled pastry. Cover and chill 2 hours or until firm.

Cut peaches into slices. Heat apricot preserves over low heat just until melted; strain. Arrange peaches and blueberries over cream. Brush with preserves. Refrigerate until serving time.

YIELD

12 bars

Per bar

calories 293, protein 3 g,
fat 13 g, sodium 142 mg,
carbohydrates 43 g,
potassium 246 mg

TIME

15 minutes preparation
30 minutes cooking
15 minutes cooling

INGREDIENTS

8 ounces pitted dates
1 cup apple juice
1 cup all-purpose flour
1 cup old-fashioned rolled oats
¼ cup granulated sugar
½ cup firmly packed dark brown
    sugar
½ teaspoon baking soda
¼ teaspoon salt

½ cup + 2 teaspoons butter, at room
    temperature
⅔ cup chopped walnuts

In small saucepan, simmer dates and apple juice 5 to 10 minutes until thick, stirring often to break up dates. Cool to room temperature.

Grease and flour an 8-inch square pan. Preheat oven to 375 degrees.

In medium bowl, stir together flour, oats, granulated sugar, brown sugar, baking soda, and salt. Using pastry blender or 2 knives ①, cut in ½ cup butter until mixture resembles crumbs.

Divide mixture in half. Press half of mixture into bottom of pan ②. Spread with date mixture. Stir walnuts into remaining crumbs. Sprinkle over dates and press down lightly ③. Cut remaining 2 teaspoons butter into small pieces and dot top. Bake 30 minutes.

YIELD

8 servings

Per serving (without sherbet)
calories 123, protein 1 g, carbohydrates 31 g, potassium 241 mg

TIME

25 minutes preparation
3 to 5 minutes cooking

INGREDIENTS

1 large white grapefruit
1 large pink grapefruit
1 orange
1 can (8 ounces) pineapple chunks, in juice
1 pear
1 can (8¾ ounces) dark sweet cherries, or 1 cup fresh cherries
⅓ cup granulated sugar

½ teaspoon ground ginger
2 tablespoons honey
2 cups lemon sherbet (optional)

Over a medium bowl to catch the juices, peel the grapefruits and orange and divide into sections ①. Add pineapple and juice to bowl. Cut pear into slices. Add to bowl, making sure each slice gets coated with juice. Drain cherries and add cherries to bowl; discard juice. Drain fruits in bowl, reserving juice. Arrange fruits in a wide shallow bowl or on a platter.

In large skillet, stir sugar and ginger together. Add ⅔ cup of the fruit juices and honey to skillet. Cook over low heat, stirring until sugar is dissolved. Bring to a boil. Boil, stirring occasionally, 3 to 5 minutes until thickened and reduced to about ½ cup ②. Pour over fruit ③. Serve with lemon sherbet, if desired.

YIELD

10 servings

Per serving
calories 130, protein 3 g,
fat 10 g, sodium 18 mg,
carbohydrates 7 g,
potassium 154 mg

TIME

20 minutes preparation
5 to 6 hours freezing

INGREDIENTS

1 envelope unflavored gelatin
1/4 cup water
1/2 cup cream of coconut
2 egg yolks
3 cups fresh strawberries or frozen
   strawberries, thawed
1/2 teaspoon rum extract
2 egg whites
1 tablespoon granulated sugar

1/2 cup heavy cream
1/4 cup shredded coconut
1/2 cup sliced strawberries

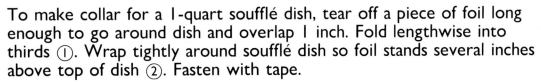

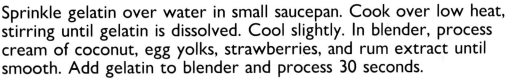

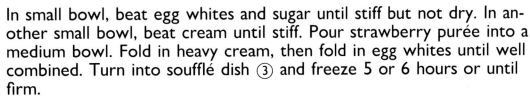

To make collar for a 1-quart soufflé dish, tear off a piece of foil long enough to go around dish and overlap 1 inch. Fold lengthwise into thirds ①. Wrap tightly around soufflé dish so foil stands several inches above top of dish ②. Fasten with tape.

Sprinkle gelatin over water in small saucepan. Cook over low heat, stirring until gelatin is dissolved. Cool slightly. In blender, process cream of coconut, egg yolks, strawberries, and rum extract until smooth. Add gelatin to blender and process 30 seconds.

In small bowl, beat egg whites and sugar until stiff but not dry. In another small bowl, beat cream until stiff. Pour strawberry purée into a medium bowl. Fold in heavy cream, then fold in egg whites until well combined. Turn into soufflé dish ③ and freeze 5 or 6 hours or until firm.

Before serving, remove from freezer and take collar off soufflé dish. Garnish with coconut and sliced strawberries.

COCONUT MERINGUES WITH CHOCOLATE MOUSSE

YIELD

6 servings

Per serving
calories 344, protein 4 g,
fat 20 g, sodium 142 mg,
carbohydrates 39 g,
potassium 109 mg

TIME

25 minutes preparation
1 hour cooking
30 minutes cooling
4 hours chilling

INGREDIENTS

2 egg whites, at room temperature
¼ teaspoon cream of tartar
⅛ teaspoon salt
½ teaspoon vanilla extract
½ cup granulated sugar
½ cup shredded coconut

MOUSSE

3 ounces semisweet chocolate
1 egg
2 egg yolks
⅓ cup granulated sugar
3 tablespoons butter, at room
    temperature
⅓ cup heavy cream

Lightly grease and flour a baking sheet. Preheat oven to 275 degrees. In medium bowl, beat egg whites, cream of tartar, and salt until soft ①. Beat in vanilla and sugar, 1 tablespoon at a time, until stiff and glossy. Fold in coconut. Pipe or spoon onto baking sheet forming nests ②. Bake 1 hour. Cool completely.

In small saucepan, melt chocolate over low heat; cool slightly. In medium bowl, beat egg, egg yolks, and sugar until thick, about 5 minutes. Gradually beat in chocolate. Beat in butter, 1 tablespoon at a time, beating 2 minutes after each addition.

In small bowl, beat cream until thick. Fold into chocolate mixture ③. Spoon mixture into meringue shells and chill at least 4 hours.

YIELD

18 bar cookies

Per cookie

calories 192, protein 2 g,
fat 8 g, sodium 113 mg,
carbohydrates 30 g,
potassium 43 mg

TIME

15 minutes preparation
35 to 40 minutes cooking

INGREDIENTS

¾ cup butter, at room temperature
½ cup granulated sugar
⅓ cup firmly packed light brown
   sugar
2 cups all-purpose flour
¼ teaspoon salt
¼ teaspoon baking soda
1 tablespoon lemon juice
¾ cup apricot preserves

Preheat oven to 375 degrees. Grease a 9-inch square baking pan. In medium bowl, beat butter until creamy. Stir in sugar and brown sugar. Add flour, salt, and baking soda. Stir until mixture is crumbly.

Set aside 1 cup crumb mixture for top; press remaining crumb mixture into baking pan ①. Stir lemon juice into apricot preserves. Spread into pan, leaving a ¼-inch border around all edges ②.

Sprinkle preserves with remaining 1 cup crumb mixture ③. Bake 35 to 40 minutes until lightly browned.

YIELD

6 servings

*Per serving
(without cake)*
calories 207, protein 1 g,
fat 6 g, sodium 63 mg,
carbohydrates 34 g,
potassium 420 mg

TIME

5 minutes preparation
10 minutes cooking

INGREDIENTS

3 tablespoons butter
1/3 cup firmly packed dark brown
   sugar
1/4 teaspoon ground cinnamon
3 tablespoons orange juice
1/4 cup spiced rum
6 small bananas
6 slices pound cake

In a large skillet, melt butter over low heat. Add brown sugar and cinnamon. Stir in orange juice and 2 tablespoons of the rum. Cook, stirring, until sugar is dissolved.

Peel bananas and cut in half lengthwise ①. Bring sugar mixture to a boil. Add bananas to skillet. Cook, about 3 minutes, basting bananas with syrup ②. Pour remaining rum over bananas ③. Serve over pound cake.

15

YIELD

6 servings

Per serving
calories 127, protein 2 g,
fat 2 g, sodium 10 mg,
carbohydrates 24 g,
potassium 404 mg

TIME

10 minutes preparation

INGREDIENTS

2 egg yolks
3 tablespoons granulated sugar
1 teaspoon lemon juice
¼ cup marsala or madeira wine
1 cup blueberries
2 peaches, sliced
2 cups cantaloupe balls
3 cups hulled strawberries

In top of double boiler, beat egg yolks and sugar until combined. Place over double boiler filled with hot, not boiling water. Beat until frothy ①.

Add lemon juice. Continue to beat, adding marsala, 1 tablespoon at a time, until sauce is smooth and thick ②. Do not overcook.

Place fruit into individual serving dishes ③. Spoon zabaglione over fruit. Serve immediately.

YIELD

12 servings

Per serving
calories 552, protein 5 g, fat 29 g, sodium 382 mg, carbohydrates 70 g, potassium 181 mg

TIME

20 minutes preparation
35 to 40 minutes cooking
1 hour cooling

INGREDIENTS

2 cups all-purpose flour
2/3 cup unsweetened cocoa
2 teaspoons baking soda
1/2 teaspoon salt
3/4 cup butter, at room temperature
1 1/2 cups granulated sugar
2 teaspoons vanilla extract
2 eggs
1/2 cup water
8 ounces sour cream

ICING

3/4 cup butter, at room temperature
1/3 cup unsweetened cocoa
1 teaspoon vanilla extract
2 tablespoons sour cream
2 1/2 cups confectioners sugar

Grease two 9-inch round layer cake pans. Line with wax paper ①, grease again, then flour. Preheat oven to 350 degrees. Sift flour with cocoa, baking soda, and salt.

In a medium bowl, beat butter until creamy. Add sugar and vanilla; beat until smooth. Beat in eggs. Add 1 cup of the flour mixture; beat until blended. Beat in water and sour cream. Add remaining flour mixture and beat until blended. Divide batter between pans ② and bake 35 to 40 minutes until a cake tester inserted in center comes out clean. Cool in pans on wire racks 10 minutes. Remove from pans to wire racks. Remove wax paper from bottoms of cakes ③ and cool completely.

In small bowl, beat butter and cocoa until smooth. Add vanilla and sour cream. Gradually add sugar, beating until icing is smooth and creamy. Spread the bottom of one layer of cake with icing. Top with second layer. Spread remaining icing over top and sides of cake.

YIELD

6 servings

Per serving
calories 372, protein 9 g,
fat 11 g, sodium 119 mg,
carbohydrates 59 g,
potassium 405 mg

TIME

15 minutes preparation
45 minutes cooking
9 to 10 hours chilling

INGREDIENTS

½ cup granulated sugar
¼ cup water
3 eggs
½ teaspoon almond extract
½ teaspoon vanilla extract
⅔ cup orange juice
1 can (14 ounces) sweetened
   condensed milk
⅔ cup water
¼ cup sliced almonds
6 orange slices, cut in half

Preheat oven to 350 degrees. In medium saucepan, stir sugar and ¼ cup water over low heat until sugar dissolves. Increase heat to high and boil, without stirring, 4 to 5 minutes until golden. Pour into 4-cup ring mold. Holding ring mold with a potholder, tilt, and turn to coat sides with caramelized sugar ①.

In medium bowl, lightly beat eggs with almond extract and vanilla. Stir in orange juice, condensed milk, and ⅔ cup water. Pour into ring mold over caramel. Place ring mold in a baking pan and fill pan with enough hot water to come halfway up side of mold ②. Using potholders, carefully place pan in oven, being careful not to let water spill. Bake 45 minutes or until a knife inserted halfway between edge and center of custard comes out clean. Remove custard from water to wire rack and let cool 1 hour. Chill 8 hours or until serving time.

To serve, run a knife around edges between custard and ring mold. Place a plate over bottom of mold. Invert and shake to remove custard ③. Garnish with almonds and orange slices.

TOFFEE NUT BARS

YIELD

12 bars

Per bar
calories 218, protein 2 g,
fat 16 g, sodium 97 mg,
carbohydrates 17 g,
potassium 57 mg

TIME

20 minutes preparation
16 minutes cooking
15 minutes cooling

INGREDIENTS

¼ cup butter, at room temperature
¼ cup granulated sugar
1 teaspoon vanilla extract
¾ cup all-purpose flour
¼ teaspoon baking powder
¾ cup chopped chocolate-covered
    toffee bars (three 2½-ounce bars)
¼ cup chopped almonds

Preheat oven to 375 degrees. Grease and flour an 8-inch square pan. In a small bowl, beat butter, sugar, and vanilla until creamy. Fold in flour and baking powder, cutting through mixture until it resembles crumbs. Place mixture in pan and pat down ①. Bake 8 minutes.

Mix chopped toffee and almonds. Sprinkle mixture over bars ② and bake 8 minutes longer. Cool on wire rack ③. Cut into 12 bars.

LEMON CREAM PIE

YIELD

8 servings

Per serving
calories 258, protein 3 g,
fat 14 g, sodium 131 mg,
carbohydrates 31 g,
potassium 119 mg

TIME

15 minutes preparation
2 to 3 hours chilling

INGREDIENTS

¾ cup graham cracker crumbs
3 tablespoons granulated sugar
3 tablespoons butter, melted

FILLING

1 envelope unflavored gelatin
¼ cup water
¾ cup heavy cream
⅔ cup granulated sugar
2 teaspoons grated lemon peel

⅓ cup lemon juice
1 cup plain yogurt
5 lemon slices

In small bowl, mix graham cracker crumbs and sugar. Stir in butter ①. Press mixture into bottom of an 8-inch springform pan ②.

Sprinkle gelatin over water in small saucepan. Cook over low heat, stirring until gelatin is dissolved. Remove from heat and cool slightly.

Beat heavy cream and sugar until stiff. Stir lemon peel, lemon juice, and yogurt into gelatin. Fold lemon mixture into whipped cream ③. Turn into springform pan. Cover and refrigerate until set, 2 to 3 hours. Just before serving, cut halfway through lemon slices and garnish pie with twisted lemon slices.

YIELD

8 servings

Per sandwich
calories 439, protein 6 g,
fat 22 g, sodium 250 mg,
carbohydrates 57 g,
potassium 282 mg

TIME

20 minutes preparation
10 to 12 minutes cooking
20 minutes cooling
3 to 4 hours freezing

INGREDIENTS

½ cup butter, at room temperature
¾ cup firmly packed light brown
   sugar
2 teaspoons water
½ teaspoon vanilla extract
1½ cups old-fashioned rolled oats
¾ cup all-purpose flour
½ teaspoon baking soda
¼ teaspoon salt
2⅔ cups ice cream

GLAZE

3 ounces semisweet chocolate
5 tablespoons milk

Preheat oven to 350 degrees. In medium bowl, beat butter and sugar until light. Beat in water and vanilla. Stir in oats, flour, baking soda, and salt until combined.

Using about 1½ tablespoons dough for each cookie, roll mixture into 16 balls ①. Place on greased baking sheet and flatten to about 3-inch rounds ②. Bake 10 to 12 minutes. Let cool on baking sheet about 2 minutes. Remove to wire rack and cool completely.

Place ⅓ cup ice cream on bottom of each of 8 cookies. Top with remaining 8 cookies ③. Wrap in clear plastic wrap and freeze about 2 hours or until firm.

In small saucepan, melt chocolate in milk over low heat, stirring constantly. Let mixture cool slightly. Line a baking sheet with waxed paper. Unwrap sandwiches and dip each one partially into chocolate, then place on waxed paper. Return to freezer and freeze 1 to 2 hours, until glaze has hardened. Wrap in clear plastic wrap.

YIELD

8 servings

Per serving

calories 377, protein 4 g,
fat 17 g, sodium 372 mg,
carbohydrates 52 g,
potassium 147 mg

TIME

15 minutes preparation
35 to 40 minutes cooking
5 minutes cooling

INGREDIENTS

½ cup + 3 tablespoons butter, at
  room temperature
1 can (11 ounces) mandarin orange
  sections
1 can (8 ounces) pineapple rings
⅓ cup firmly packed light brown
  sugar
⅔ cup granulated sugar
2 eggs
½ teaspoon vanilla extract

1⅓ cups all-purpose flour
1 teaspoon baking powder
½ teaspoon salt
⅓ cup milk

Preheat oven to 350 degrees. Place 3 tablespoons butter in a 9-inch round cake pan. Place pan in oven until butter is melted. Drain oranges and pineapple slices on paper towels ①. Arrange in bottom of pan. Sprinkle with brown sugar ②.

In medium bowl, beat remaining ½ cup butter and sugar until creamy. Add eggs and vanilla. Stir in flour, baking powder, and salt. Stir in milk. Spread batter over fruit ③. Bake 35 to 40 minutes until cake tester inserted in center comes out clean.

Let stand 5 minutes. Run a knife around edge of cake. Place a plate over cake and pan and invert. Remove pan.

YIELD

10 servings

Per serving
calories 455, protein 6 g,
fat 36 g, sodium 196 mg,
carbohydrates 32 g,
potassium 247 mg

TIME

25 minutes preparation
3 hours chilling

INGREDIENTS

⅔ cup finely chopped pecans or
  walnuts
⅓ cup tea cookie crumbs
¼ cup granulated sugar
¼ cup butter, melted

FILLING

½ cup butter, at room temperature
¾ cup granulated sugar
2 teaspoons vanilla extract
3 ounces unsweetened chocolate,
  melted

⅛ teaspoon salt
3 eggs
¼ cup sliced almonds
¼ cup chopped pecans or walnuts
¾ cup grated white chocolate
  (2 ounces)
½ cup pecan or walnut halves

Stir together chopped pecans, crumbs, and sugar. Stir in butter ①. Press mixture into a 9-inch pie plate.

For filling, in large bowl beat butter, sugar, and vanilla until light and fluffy. Beat in chocolate and salt. Add eggs, one at a time, beating 3 minutes after each egg ②. Stir in almonds and pecans. Fold in white chocolate. Spoon mixture into pie shell, mounding in center ③. Cover and refrigerate several hours. Garnish with pecan halves.

YIELD

4 servings

Per pear
calories 457, protein 2 g,
fat 11 g, sodium 101 mg,
carbohydrates 78 g,
potassium 262 mg

TIME

20 minutes preparation
10 to 15 minutes cooking
3 hours chilling

INGREDIENTS

4 pears
1½ cups water
¾ cup granulated sugar
3 strips orange peel
¼ cup cognac

FILLING

3 ounces cream cheese
1 teaspoon cognac

SAUCE

2 tablespoons dark brown sugar
1 tablespoon butter
2 tablespoons light corn syrup
2 tablespoons cognac

Peel pears and cut in half. Using a melon baller, scoop out seeds ①. Cut a small slice from the bottom of each pear ②.

In large skillet, stir together water, sugar, and orange peel. Cook over low heat, stirring constantly until sugar dissolves. Bring to boil and boil 3 minutes. Stir in ¼ cup cognac. Add pears. Cover and simmer over low heat 10 to 15 minutes until tender. Remove from heat. Uncover and let pears cool in syrup 15 minutes. Remove pears to plate and chill several hours. Reserve syrup.

In small bowl, beat cream cheese with 1 teaspoon cognac. Drain pears on paper towels. Spread cream cheese mixture onto 4 pear halves ③. Top with matching pear halves.

Stir brown sugar into syrup until dissolved. Bring to a boil; boil 5 minutes. Remove from heat and stir in butter, corn syrup, and cognac. Serve warm or chilled over pears.

24

YIELD

8 servings

Per serving
calories 496, protein 8 g,
fat 25 g, sodium 423 mg,
carbohydrates 61 g,
potassium 202 mg

TIME

25 minutes preparation
3 to 5 hours freezing
1 hour, 5 minutes cooking
10 minutes cooling

INGREDIENTS

$^2/_3$ cup butter, at room temperature
$^3/_4$ cup granulated sugar
3 eggs
1 teaspoon vanilla extract
1 cup all-purpose flour
$^1/_2$ teaspoon baking powder
$^1/_4$ teaspoon salt
2 pints favorite ice cream

MERINGUE

3 egg whites
$^1/_4$ teaspoon cream of tartar
$^1/_4$ teaspoon salt
$^1/_2$ cup granulated sugar

Preheat oven to 325 degrees. Grease and flour an 8½ × 4½ × 2½-inch loaf pan. In medium bowl, beat butter and sugar until creamy.

Beat in eggs and vanilla. Add remaining ingredients except ice cream and beat until blended. Spread in prepared pan. Bake about 1 hour until a cake tester inserted in center comes out clean. Cool in pan on wire rack 10 minutes. Run a knife around edge of cake, remove from pan, and cool completely.

Let ice cream soften slightly. Cut a slice off top of cake to level off, if necessary ①. Cut cake in half horizontally ②. Spread 1 pint of ice cream between layers. Spread remaining 1 pint of ice cream on top of cake ③. Wrap tightly and freeze several hours or until solid.

Preheat oven to 450 degrees. To make meringue, beat egg whites, cream of tartar, and salt until soft peaks form when beaters are lifted. Beat in sugar, 1 tablespoon at a time, beating until very stiff and glossy, about 5 minutes.

Place cake on a cookie sheet. Spread sides and top of cake completely with meringue. Bake 5 minutes until lightly browned. Serve immediately.

NOTE *A commercially prepared pound cake about 8 inches long may be used in recipe instead of homemade pound cake.*

YIELD

10 servings

Per serving
calories 292, protein 3 g,
fat 11 g, sodium 194 mg,
carbohydrates 46 g,
potassium 198 mg

TIME

20 minutes preparation
25 minutes cooking
1 hour cooling

INGREDIENTS

½ cup + 3 tablespoons granulated
    sugar
1 cup all-purpose flour
1 ¼ teaspoons baking soda
¼ teaspoon salt
3 egg yolks
¼ cup butter, melted
¼ cup molasses
2 tablespoons water
1 tablespoon ground ginger
2 teaspoons ground cinnamon

1 teaspoon ground cloves
3 egg whites

FILLING

6 cups chopped, pared apples (4 large
    apples)
¼ cup butter
½ teaspoon ground cinnamon
⅓ cup granulated sugar
¼ cup water

Preheat oven to 375 degrees. Grease a 17 × 11 × 1-inch jellyroll pan. Line with waxed paper. Grease waxed paper and sprinkle with 1 tablespoon sugar and 1 tablespoon flour.

Sift together remaining flour, baking soda, and salt. Beat egg yolks with the ½ cup sugar, melted butter, molasses, water, ginger, cinnamon, and cloves until thick about 3 minutes. Fold in flour mixture.

Beat egg whites until stiff. Fold into batter. Spread into prepared pan. Bake 12 minutes until firm to the touch. While cake is baking, sprinkle a clean kitchen towel with 1 tablespoon sugar.

Let cake stand 1 minute. Loosen edges from pan and invert cake onto towel. Peel off waxed paper ① (if cake sticks, slide a knife between cake and waxed paper to separate). Sprinkle top of cake with 1 tablespoon sugar. Roll up cake and towel ②. Place seam side down on wire rack and cool completely.

For filling, mix all ingredients in medium saucepan. Cover and cook over medium-low heat, stirring occasionally, 12 to 15 minutes until tender. Uncover and cook, stirring constantly to break up pieces of apple, 3 to 5 minutes until liquid has evaporated. Cool.

Unroll cake. Spread with apple mixture ③. Reroll cake, removing towel. Refrigerate until serving time.

CRANBERRY ORANGE SORBET

YIELD

12 servings

Per serving
calories 86, sodium 1 mg,
carbohydrates 22 g,
potassium 118 mg

TIME

15 minutes preparation
8 to 10 minutes cooking
3 to 4 hours freezing

INGREDIENTS

1 cup water
¾ cup granulated sugar
4 slices lemon peel
2 cups orange juice
1 cup apple juice
2 cups whole fresh or frozen
   cranberries
1 teaspoon grated orange peel

In small saucepan, stir together water and sugar. Add slices of lemon peel. Cook over low heat, stirring, until sugar is completely dissolved. Bring to boil and boil, without stirring, for 8 to 10 minutes until mixture is reduced to about ½ cup. Remove mixture from heat and let cool slightly.

Mix orange juice and apple juice in blender ①. Add cranberries and orange peel. Process about 1 minute until mixture is almost smooth. Remove lemon peel from syrup. Add syrup to blender and process 30 seconds or until completely mixed in. Pour into metal bowl ②, cover, and freeze 30 to 45 minutes until ice begins to form.

Beat mixture, breaking up ice ③. Cover and return to freezer for about 1 hour. Beat, breaking up ice crystals. Return to freezer until solid, about 1 to 2 hours. Before serving, let sorbet stand at room temperature 15 to 20 minutes.

YIELD

6 servings

Per serving
calories 370, protein 8 g,
fat 19 g, sodium 343 mg,
carbohydrates 44 g,
potassium 287 mg

TIME

15 minutes preparation
45 to 50 minutes cooking

INGREDIENTS

6 to 7 slices stale bread
2 eggs
¾ cup granulated sugar
⅓ cup unsweetened cocoa
1 teaspoon ground cinnamon
¾ teaspoon vanilla extract
¼ cup butter, melted
¼ teaspoon salt
2½ cups milk
⅓ cup heavy cream
1 tablespoon confectioners sugar

Preheat oven to 350 degrees. Grease a 9½-inch oval baking dish (5½ to 6 cups). Cut crusts off bread. Cut bread into ½- to ¾-inch cubes to make 5 cups ①.

In medium bowl, beat eggs, sugar, cocoa, cinnamon, and ½ teaspoon vanilla until blended. Beat in butter and salt. Gradually stir in milk ②. Add bread, stirring to break up cubes ③. Pour into dish. Bake 45 to 50 minutes, until a knife inserted in center comes out clean.

In small bowl, beat heavy cream, confectioners sugar, and remaining ¼ teaspoon vanilla until stiff. Serve over bread pudding.

YIELD

8 servings

Per serving
calories 211, protein 2 g,
fat 15 g, sodium 116 mg,
carbohydrates 17 g,
potassium 60 mg

TIME

10 minutes preparation
15 minutes cooking

INGREDIENTS

½ cup butter, at room temperature
¼ cup confectioners sugar
¼ teaspoon vanilla extract
1 cup all-purpose flour
⅓ cup ground hazelnuts
16 whole hazelnuts

28

Preheat oven to 375 degrees. Beat butter, confectioners sugar, and vanilla until creamy. Fold in flour and ground nuts. Knead slightly, forming a ball ①.

Place dough on surface that has been dusted with confectioners sugar. Flatten slightly ②, then roll into an 8-inch circle ③. Place on ungreased baking sheet.

Cutting only halfway through dough, cut circle into 8 pie-shaped pieces. Decorate with whole hazelnuts. Bake 15 minutes; cool on wire rack.

YIELD

16 servings

Per serving
calories 363, protein 5 g,
fat 17 g, sodium 148 mg,
carbohydrates 47 g,
potassium 165 mg

TIME

15 minutes preparation
1 hour cooking
10 minutes cooling

INGREDIENTS

3 cups + 1 tablespoon all-purpose
   flour
1 teaspoon baking soda
1 teaspoon baking powder
3/4 cup butter, at room temperature
1 1/2 cups granulated sugar
3 eggs
2 teaspoons vanilla extract
1 cup chopped dates
8 ounces sour cream

1 cup chopped walnuts
1 tablespoon confectioners sugar

Preheat oven to 350 degrees. Grease and flour a 9-inch springform pan with a tube bottom. Stir together 3 cups flour, baking soda, and baking powder. Beat butter and sugar until creamy. Beat in eggs and vanilla.

Toss dates with remaining 1 tablespoon flour ①. Alternately beat flour and sour cream into butter mixture. Fold in dates and walnuts ②. Turn into prepared pan. Bake 55 to 65 minutes until cake springs back when lightly touched.

Immediately remove side of pan. Cool cake 10 minutes. Remove bottom and cool cake on wire rack. Place confectioners sugar in strainer and sprinkle over cake ③.

INDEX